Animal
Chemical Combat
Poisons, Smells, and Slime

Susan K. Mitchell

Enslow Publishers, Inc.
40 Industrial Road
Box 398
Berkeley Heights, NJ 07922
USA

http://www.enslow.com

These books are dedicated to Emily, who inspired the author.

Library of Congress Cataloging-in-Publication Data
Mitchell, Susan K.
  Animal chemical combat : poisons, smells, and slime / Susan K. Mitchell.
      p. cm. — (Amazing animal defenses)
  Includes bibliographical references.
  Summary: "Readers will learn how animals defend themselves using a variety of weapons including poisons and scents"—Provided by publisher.
  ISBN 978-0-7660-3294-1
  1. Animal chemical defenses—Juvenile literature. I. Title.
  QL759.M575 2009
  591.47—dc22

                                        2008011450
ISBN-10: 0-7660-3294-9

Printed in the United States of America

10 9 8 7 6 5 4 3 2 1

To Our Readers:
We have done our best to make sure all Internet Addresses in this book were active and appropriate when we went to press. However, the author and the publisher have no control over and assume no liability for the material available on those Internet sites or on other Web sites they may link to. Any comments or suggestions can be sent by e-mail to comments@enslow.com or to the address on the back cover.

♻ Enslow Publishers, Inc., is committed to printing our books on recycled paper. The paper in every book contains 10% to 30% post-consumer waste (PCW). The cover board on the outside of each book contains 100% PCW. Our goal is to do our part to help young people and the environment too!

Cover photo: plasmatic/iStockphoto
Interior photos: Alamy/Papilio, pp. 4, 8; Alamy/Amazon-Images, p. 10; Alamy/Norman Tomalin, p. 14; Alamy/blickwinkel, pp. 22, 27, 36; Alamy/Kevin Schafer, p. 25; Alamy/MshieldsPhotos, p. 26; Alamy/Peter Arnold, Inc., p. 33; Alamy/Roger Eritja, p. 34; Alamy/The Print Collector, p. 43; Animals Animals–Earth Scenes/Patti Murray, p. 24; Animals Animals–Earth Scenes/George Bryce, p. 31; Animals Animals–Earth Scenes/Zigmund Leszczynski, p. 39; Birdforum/Mali B. Halls, p. 11; Corbis/Brandon D. Cole, pp. 40, 41; Department of Defense/SRA Rick A. Bloom, USAF, p. 44; Getty/Tom Brakefield, p. 15; Getty/ Geoff Brightling, p. 35; Getty/National Geographic, p. 38; iStockphoto/plasmatic, p. 1; iStockphoto/Cathy Keifer, p. 6; iStockphoto/Holly Kuchera, p. 12; iStockphoto/Mark Kostich, p. 20; Oxford Scientific/Satoshi Kuribayashi, p. 28; Photo Researchers, Inc./Steve Maslowski, p. 16; Visuals Unlimited/Dr. Gilbert Twiest, p. 19.

Contents

Chapter 1 Stinging, Stinky, Sticky Stuff

In the animal world, hidden weapons can be a great defense. And no weapon is easier to hide than a chemical weapon. Even the smallest of animals can pack a punch if they have poison!

Chemicals are found everywhere. They are in plants, water, and air. They are in animals, too. Most chemicals used by animals are harmless. But a few of them can be very

A copperhead's deadly chemical weapon is called venom. Snakes use venom for defense and to kill prey.

dangerous. They can cause sickness or even death if touched or eaten.

There are many ways that chemicals help keep an animal safe. Some are smelly. Some are just plain sticky. And then there are those deadly ones. Some animals use poisons, also known as toxins, to protect themselves. These chemical defenses can often be very strange. But no matter how weird they may seem, chemical defenses can protect animals from being eaten.

You Are What You Eat

There are two ways that an animal can get the chemicals it needs for defense. The first way is through the food it eats. By eating plants or insects that contain poison, some animals become toxic (poisonous) themselves. The monarch butterfly is a good example. It has no way to produce its own poison. Its caterpillar

5

A monarch caterpillar (left) becomes toxic from eating milkweed. It stays toxic even after it becomes a butterfly (right).

babies are not born toxic. They get that way only after they start eating milkweed.

The milkweed plant is poisonous to many animals. Monarch caterpillars are able to eat it safely, however. In fact, it is the only food that a monarch caterpillar eats. The poisons of the milkweed plant stay stored inside the caterpillar's body.

When the caterpillar changes into a monarch butterfly, these chemicals make the butterfly taste terrible. Any predator that tries to take a bite of the monarch butterfly will become very sick.

The second way that an animal can have a chemical defense is to make the chemical inside its own body. All animals make some kinds of chemicals, which are used simply to keep their bodies working. Some digest food. Others carry oxygen through the body. Chemicals do many jobs. Most of them are not dangerous at all. But some animals are able to make dangerous chemicals.

These poisons are produced by glands in the animal's body. They are stored in the glands until the animal uses them in an attack. For the unfortunate predator who comes across them,

Nice to Smell You

One important type of chemical used by animals are pheromones (FAIR-a-mones). Pheromones are made by an animal's own body. Other animals can detect pheromones by their smell. These chemicals work like a kind of language for animals. They are used to send many different types of messages, which are picked up only by other animals.

Pheromones can help an animal find a mate. They can warn other animals when predators are close. Some pheromones can also mark an animal's

living and hunting area. Animals often rub against trees or bushes where they live. They might also spray objects with fluids from their bodies. This rubbing and spraying leaves tiny bits of scent behind. By leaving their scent with pheromones, animals warn others to stay away.

most poisons simply cause itching or burning. But others can kill.

Using chemical weapons can be pretty tricky. To use their weapons, animals often have to get close to a predator. This, of course, is very dangerous. So each animal that makes its own chemical weapon has to have a good way to deliver it. Some have body parts that spray chemicals at their enemies. In others, the chemicals ooze from the skin. No matter how an animal delivers its chemical defense, the goal is to get away alive.

A Bright Idea!

Many animals need to hide from predators using camouflage. They often have dull colors to help them blend in with nature. Animals with chemical defenses do not have to worry about that. They often walk, hop, swim, or climb around in plain sight. Many of them advertise their chemical defenses with skin that is brightly colored. In nature, the more

9

A poison dart frog's bright colors are a warning to predators to stay away.

colorful an animal is, the more likely that it is very poisonous.

These bright colors warn predators to stay away. Over time, predators have learned that these animals are not good to eat. It only takes a few match-ups with a stinky, bad tasting, or slimy animal to teach predators a lesson. Chemical defenses can really do the trick!

*Wild*FACT Some poison dart frogs have a poison so strong that less than two micrograms of it could kill any predator. That is less poison than would fit in the period at the end of a sentence!

Special Delivery

Very few birds have chemical defenses. In fact, there are only two known birds whose bodies are actually poisonous. One is the hooded pitohui (PIT-oo-wee). The other is called the ifrita. Both birds live in New Guinea. Their feathers and skin are very toxic. Scientists believe that some of the things they eat make them poisonous.

Other birds use chemical weapons, but their bodies are not toxic. And some have weird ways of delivering their defensive chemicals. The fulmar (below) is one of these. When it is threatened, this bird vomits an oily chemical at its attacker. This oil can seriously damage the feathers of other birds. The fulmar can launch its gross weapon up to five feet!

Chapter 2

That Stinks!

There is no mistaking when a skunk has been in a scuffle. If a skunk has to defend itself, it can get pretty stinky! That is because skunks use smelly chemicals for protection. Most animals know enough to stay away from them. Even large animals are no match for the powerful stink of a skunk.

To a curious bear cub, a skunk might look interesting. But if the skunk feels threatened enough to use its stinky weapon, watch out!

Skunks are small mammals. There are many different kinds of skunks. They can be striped or spotted. Some skunks, like the hog-nosed skunk, have an all-white back. No matter how it looks, that black-and-white coloring tells other animals to stay far away!

A skunk's chemical weapon is located on its rear end. There are two tiny holes below the base of the skunk's tail. Inside each hole is a tiny sac called a scent gland. The scent glands are full of a stinky, oily chemical. When a skunk is threatened, it turns, aims, and fires! It squeezes tiny muscles that cause a jet of yellow oil to squirt out of the holes. That oil is super stinky. Skunks can carefully control their squirting. They can spray a fine mist or a thick jet stream.

They are pretty good at aiming, too. A skunk does not just shoot anywhere. It tries to aim at the face of a predator. That is because

Take It Slow, Loris

There are many poisonous animals in the world, **but** very few of them are mammals. The slow loris is one. This animal is closely related to monkeys and apes. Like its name says, the slow loris is a very slow-moving animal. It lives in trees. It also has giant eyes. These big eyes help the slow loris hunt for insects at night.

On the inside of the slow loris's elbow is a small gland. It produces a poison that smells like

stinky gym socks. The slow loris uses the poison in a couple of ways. It can rub the poison on its teeth so it will have a toxic bite. The slow loris also rubs the smelly toxin on a baby loris's fur. This makes the baby loris instantly poisonous. Then the baby is protected from predators while the parents are out hunting.

A skunk raises its tail to take aim.

the chemical is not just stinky. It stings and burns. This stops the predator long enough for the skunk to run away and hide. Skunks are so good at aiming that they get almost no stinky oil on themselves. Even skunks do not like to smell like skunk!

Wild FACT Skunks do not just have their own chemical defenses. They can also survive chemical attacks dished out by other animals. For example, a skunk can often survive a snakebite that would kill another animal.

Shy Little Stinkers

Skunks use their secret chemical weapon only as a last resort. They are actually very shy animals. Most skunks live in burrows or dens.

Skunks use their great sense of smell to sniff out food. These eggs were a good find!

They are not very picky about where they live. Any hollow log can make a great den for a skunk. As long as it can hide, a skunk feels safe. Sometimes they even share their burrows with other small mammals. Skunks spend most of the day hiding and resting. They are usually nocturnal, which means they are active at night. After the sun goes down, skunks come out to hunt for food.

Smell is everything to a skunk. Not only can a skunk smell bad, but its own sense of smell is fantastic. Since skunks do not see very well, they use their nose to find food. Skunks sniff along looking for hidden bugs and other treats. They have been known to sniff out food that is several inches underground.

A Bug-Proof Fur Coat

Poison can keep predators away. It can also keep away other, less deadly pests like mites and fleas. Many mammals use the poisons of plants and other animals on their own fur. For example, some kinds of monkeys rub crushed millipedes on their fur. Millipedes are animals related to insects with many legs and long bodies made up of several segments.

Some millipedes are pretty toxic. So, when monkeys rub them on themselves, scientists believe they are using the millipedes as a sort of insect repellent. The poisons of millipedes and other bugs help keep pesky mites and fleas out of the monkeys' fur.

Birds have also been known to do the same thing. Some birds will rub ants on their feathers. The ants give off a poison that helps keep the birds' feathers clean and pest-free.

All a Big Act

During daytime naps or nighttime hunts, a skunk can often run into trouble. Large predators like coyotes or bobcats may get curious and stop to check out a skunk. If the skunk feels threatened, it has several tricks to use before it fires a stink bomb.

The first thing a skunk will do is try to bluff the predator. This means the skunk puts on a show to look and sound meaner than it really is. Skunks raise their tail high and puff out their fur. They stamp their feet while they growl and hiss. Hopefully, this will be enough to scare the predator away.

If the bluff does not work, the spotted skunk will even do a handstand! It stands on its front paws with its back legs and tail high in the air. This helps it look larger. It also helps the skunk get a good aim if the bluff is not working. If the predator does not back off after all this, it is time to use the secret chemical weapon.

Wild FACT

A skunk's spray is an oily chemical. And since oil and water do not mix, water will not wash it away. Some people say that using baking soda and dish detergent is the best way to get rid of the smell on people or pets.

Even a large dog is no match for the well-armed skunk. Most animals have learned over time to leave skunks alone.

Whether the skunk is standing on its front paws or on all fours, it first turns its backside to the enemy. Then it fires its stinky stream of skunk oil. The scent glands full of oil are very small. Only a tiny bit of smelly oil is made. But it is more than enough! The smell alone is usually enough to make most predators run away.

Chapter 3

Pretty but Poisonous

Deep in the tropical rain forests of South America is a rainbow of tiny, colorful frogs. They are called poison dart frogs. Their bright colors are for more than just looks. They warn other animals that the poison dart frog can be very dangerous.

A poison dart frog's color makes it beautiful to look at, and its tiny size makes it "cute." But most are toxic, and some are deadly!

Even the largest poison dart frog is only a couple of inches long. These little frogs pack quite a punch, however. Inside their skin are poison glands. This poisonous skin is how the frogs got their name. Native tribes who live in the jungles often rubbed the tips of their darts on the frog's skin. This coated their darts with poison. They used the deadly darts to hunt for food.

Some poison dart frogs have poison that just tastes bad to predators. Others have poison that causes burning and stinging when it is eaten. And there are a few poison dart frogs that are truly deadly. One of these is the golden poison dart frog. This bright golden-yellow frog is one of the most poisonous animals in the world. It has a strong enough poison in its skin to kill a human.

Poison dart frogs are not born poisonous. The poison comes mostly from the food they eat.

Scientists think that it takes a whole "chain" of food to give the poison dart frog its poison. For example, insects in the jungle eat plants that produce toxic substances. The plant's poison is then in the insect. Then the poison dart frogs eat those insects. The poison dart frog's body allows it to eat the poison without being harmed. The poison then becomes part of the poison dart frog's body chemistry.

▼ The golden poison dart frog is one of the most poisonous animals in the world. Its toxins can kill a human.

A poison dart frog that is taken from the jungle and fed regular insects will become much less poisonous. In fact, poison dart frogs that are born in captivity (not born in the wild) never have any poison at all.

No Need to Hide

Poison dart frogs are diurnal. This means they are active during the day. They spend their days looking for ants and other insects to eat. The frogs are almost always safe from predators while they are busy hunting. Their bright colors tell predators to stay far away.

Poison dart frogs are amphibians. That means they live both in water and on land. The tiny frogs raise their young in the high trees of the rain forest. They place the baby frogs, called tadpoles, inside the bromeliad (bro-MEE-lee-ad) plants that grow in the trees.

There, the poisonous parents watch after their tadpoles. They bring small insects for them to eat. Soon the tadpoles begin to change.

Ooey, Gooey, Sticky, Gluey

Some types of frogs produce even weirder things than poison. One of them is the tomato frog. This round red frog lives only in Madagascar. It can produce a sticky liquid when it is attacked. The liquid is white and looks very much like glue. It acts like glue, also.

When threatened, the tomato frog first puffs itself up with air to look larger. If this does not

scare off the predator, special glands in the tomato frog's skin start oozing the sticky "glue." The glue is not poisonous. But this stuff is so strong that it can glue a predator's mouth shut for several days!

Scientists are experimenting with the glue of this and other oozing frogs. They hope to someday be able to help repair human joints using the sticky stuff. They may also be able to repair human cartilage, which is the material that humans' noses and ears are made of.

They lose their tails. The tadpoles' skin starts to turn bright colors. Thanks to the insects that they ate, the skin of the young poison dart frogs is also now poisonous.

Different Chemical Warfare

The skin of any amphibian is amazing. It helps the animal breathe. It can also produce chemicals used for defense. The bad news is, the skin can be affected by chemicals in the air and water. Scientists think of some amphibians as "indicator species." That means studying them can give good clues to what is happening in their environment. Often, amphibians are the first animals to show signs of trouble in polluted places.

Poison dart frogs raise their young in plants called bromeliads (below).

Some kinds of poison dart frogs gently carry their tadpoles on their backs to move them!

Since a poison dart frog's skin is so sensitive, it can absorb chemicals that may be in the water or air. This can cause these beautiful frogs to become sick or die. Chemical pollution can also cause the frogs to have fewer babies. By studying poison dart frogs, scientists can tell a lot about what is going on in the rain forest. Even tiny changes in the environment will affect the frogs before most other animals. No amount of poison can protect them from pollution.

Wild FACT

Poison dart frogs have only one known predator. It is a snake with the scientific name *Leimadophis epinephelus.* Poison dart frogs' toxins will usually not kill the snake. But if the toxin is strong enough, the snake could still get a little sick.

Fire Down Below!

Frogs are not the only amphibians that have poisonous bodies. Salamanders can be just as toxic. The fire salamander is one of them. The small insects and worms these salamanders eat make them toxic.

If it is threatened by a predator, a fire salamander can spray its poison if it has time. But even if the predator is already too close and chomps down on the fire salamander, it is still in for a rude surprise.

Most of the salamander's poison glands are around its head and neck. Predators usually try to grab their food by the head. When a predator does this to a fire salamander, it gets a mouth full of poison.

The burning, bad taste of the poison is usually enough to make the predator let go. This gives the fire salamander time to get away.

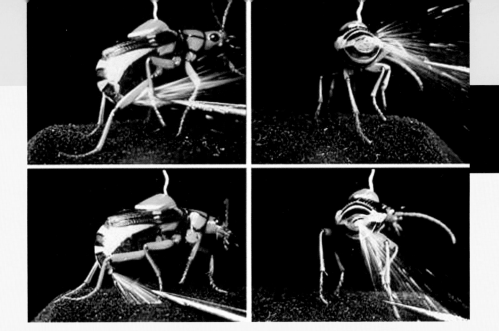

Chapter 4

Bombs Away!

The bombardier beetle may be little, but it has an amazing explosive chemical weapon. Most insects and other animals that use chemical weapons have only one defensive chemical inside their body. But the bombardier (bom-bar-DEER) beetle has two. It can mix these chemicals to cause a dramatic explosion. In the bombardier beetle, two harmless chemicals mix together to form a dangerous one.

A bombardier beetle is built like other insects. It has three body parts: a head, a thorax, and an abdomen. The abdomen of the

◀ Do not mess with the bombardier beetle. It has a chemical weapon that explodes out of its body. As shown in this scientific study, it can aim its blast in almost any direction.

bombardier beetle is where it keeps its secret weapon. Inside the beetle's abdomen, there are special cells. They store two different chemicals.

If the beetle is attacked, the cells release their chemicals into another area in the abdomen called a reservoir. The chemicals are mixed to make a dangerous weapon.

In an instant, the bombardier beetle shoots the mixed chemicals out of a small tube located behind its abdomen. This mixture is stinky and irritating. It is so hot that it actually burns when it hits its target. The heat and force of the chemicals makes some of the liquid turn to gas. The gas looks like a puff of smoke that comes out with the liquid.

There is also a loud bang when the bombardier beetle fires its weapon. The noise

Wild FACT The spray of a bombardier beetle can reach 212 degrees Fahrenheit. That is the temperature of boiling water!

alone is enough to scare most predators. But the bombardier beetle also has a great aim. Its abdomen can twist in almost any direction. This gives it dangerous accuracy when it shoots its disgusting spray at an enemy.

Ground Control

There are many kinds of bombardier beetles. They are usually about one to two inches long. Their bodies are shiny and black with red or orange markings.

Wild FACT One of the chemicals found inside the bombardier beetle is a common household chemical used to clean cuts and scratches. It is called hydrogen peroxide.

Any warm wooded or grassy area can be a good home for these beetles. Most of the day is spent hiding under rotten logs or leaves on the ground. At night, bombardier

A bombardier beetle has the same body parts as other insects, but its covered wings are not very useful for flying.

thorax

head

abdomen

elytra
(wing covers)

beetles search for food. They have wings, but they do not work well for flying. This means that the bombardier beetle cannot instantly zip off into the air. This slow-moving beetle cannot even walk away very fast! It has almost no way of escaping a predator.

Ants are the biggest threats to the bombardier beetle. But no single ant can do the job. Instead, huge numbers of ants gang up to overwhelm their prey. Hundreds of ants can take apart a large insect in a matter of minutes. For the bombardier beetle, sharing the ground

They Go Kaboom!

Most animals use their weapons to protect themselves. Some use their weapons to protect their babies, too. Very few, however, use their weapons like the exploding ants of Malaysia. These ants use their own bodies as deadly weapons to protect other ants in their colony.

When these ants are threatened, special chemicals in their body mix together just like in the bombardier beetle. When that happens, the ants explode, spraying toxins all over the place! The ant dies, but its family survives.

with these tiny hunters is dangerous business. The beetle needs a revved-up weapons system so it can stay and fight.

Complicated Chemistry

The bombardier beetle also needs its great aim when fighting against ants. Ants can attack from any direction, so the beetle needs to be able to fire its chemicals in any direction. It also needs to be able to fire more than once. In fact, the bombardier beetle can fire its weapon many times in a matter of seconds.

The bombardier beetle's chemicals are clearly dangerous. They are hot enough to burn, and they explode out of the beetle with enough force to make a loud noise. So what keeps the bombardier beetle from blowing itself to bits? The answer is another chemical reaction.

Inside the reservoir in the beetle's abdomen where the chemicals mix, other cells

▼ Ants are a bombardier beetle's worst enemy. Hundreds of ants can attack and kill a much larger beetle.

What's in a Name?

The stink bug's name says it all. It stinks! There are many kinds of stink bugs. They can be many different sizes and colors. Most stink bugs have a flattened body shaped like a shield. The one thing they all have in common is their chemical defense. If bothered, these insects can release a very smelly liquid. Few predators want to eat something that stinks.

The chemicals are kept in glands on the stink bug's thorax. It does not take much to get a stink bug to release its bad odor. They are easily bothered. A simple bump or squeeze on its sides makes the glands react. A careless human who handles a stink bug may get more than they bargained for!

This model of a bombardier beetle shows the special reservoir in its abdomen. Here, two chemicals mix with enzymes to make an explosion.

reservoir

release enzymes. There are many different kinds of enzymes. They are made naturally by all living things. An enzyme's job is to help speed up chemical reactions. The bombardier beetle's enzymes are the key to making its chemical weapon work.

When the enzymes inside the bombardier beetle mix with the chemicals, heat and pressure build up quickly. The chemicals literally explode out of the beetle's rear end. This all happens so fast that the chemicals are released before the beetle can blow itself up.

Chapter 5 Deep Sea Slime

Not all animals' chemical defenses are poisonous or smelly. Some of them are simply slimy. Slime can be a good way to get rid of predators. Few animals like being covered in disgusting gunk. The hagfish is one of the slimiest defenders on the planet. When it is bothered, it creates a giant slime cloud around itself. It can make huge amounts of the slippery stuff.

The slinky, slimy hagfish's creepy appearance has not changed in hundreds of millions of years.

Hagfish do not have scales like fish. Their skin is smooth, like an eel's skin. Some people even call hagfish "slime eels." The hagfish has been around for millions of years. In that time, the way they look has not changed. Scientists have compared ancient hagfish fossils to the hagfish of today. They look pretty much the same now as they did hundreds of millions of years ago.

The hagfish's appearance alone can be fairly frightening. They can grow to be around two feet long. They are grayish-pink in color. Hagfish do not have real eyes. They have no eye muscles or lenses. They may have only small round holes where the eyes should be. They are almost completely blind.

Wild FACT Hagfish digest their food very slowly. In fact, a hagfish might have to eat only a few times each year!

Eyes are not very important to hagfish, anyway. They often live in deep, cold water. Hagfish have been known to live as deep as 4,000 feet below the ocean's surface. At those depths, it is very dark. The hagfish relies mostly on its great senses of smell and touch to find food.

Disgusting Diet

Some of the hagfish's eating habits have given it a nasty reputation. It eats mostly marine worms and other small ocean animals. However, it

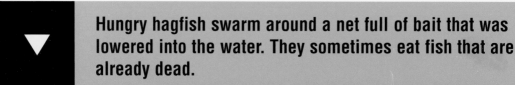

Hungry hagfish swarm around a net full of bait that was lowered into the water. They sometimes eat fish that are already dead.

Put It in Ink

Many ocean animals use ink as a chemical defense. Squids and octopuses both are able to squirt a jet of inky chemicals. This ink cloud helps distract and confuse a predator. It gives the squid or octopus time to swim to safety.

The sea hare is another ocean animal that uses ink for protection. The sea hare is a type of sea slug. It has two tentacles on its head that look a little like rabbit ears. Unlike the squid or octopus, the sea hare cannot make a speedy getaway. It is not enough for its ink to be a distraction. Instead, the sea hare's ink tastes very bad.

The chemicals in the sea hare's ink come from the algae (AL-jee) it eats (algae is a plant-like organism). The algae also gives the ink a bright purple color. The sea hare stores these chemicals in special glands. When attacked by predators, it spurts a cloud of the colorful ink. The predator gets a mouthful of the icky ink and swims away.

sometimes eats dead or dying fish. It will even burrow into the body of a sick or dying fish. Then it eats the fish from the inside out. That may be a nasty idea, but it can be very important in the ocean. By doing this, hagfish help get rid of dead material on the ocean floor. This helps keep the water clean.

Many animals like to eat hagfish. Whales, seals, and some seabirds eat hagfish. But no gilled fish hunt for hagfish. That is because of

▼ A hagfish's slime cloud can be so thick that no predator would bother trying to get through it.

the hagfish's slimy defenses. It has special glands all along its body that produce a sugary liquid if the hagfish is bothered. The liquid by itself is only a little bit slimy. When it hits salty seawater, it turns to thick slime.

There are also tiny thread-like fibers inside the slime. These tiny fibers help to make the slime extra thick and gooey. A frightened hagfish does not make a little bit of slime—it makes it by the bucketful!

Any fish caught in this huge slime ball would soon be unable to breathe. The slime would coat its gills and the fish would suffocate. But what about the hagfish's gills? How does the hagfish keep from suffocating itself in a cloud of slime? It ties itself up in a knot.

Hagfish slime is gross, but not poisonous.

By twisting itself into a knot, the hagfish can squeeze off its own slime. It slides the knot down its entire body. This wipes the slime away from the hagfish's gills. A hagfish also sneezes to get the slime out of its mouth, and to help wipe the slime away from its tiny eyes and one small nostril. This way the hagfish does not die in its own slimy defenses.

Understanding Chemical Combat

The chemical world can be complex and pretty hard to understand. Maybe it is because so many chemicals can do so many different things. The chemicals used by animals for defense are some of the wildest. They may be stinging, sticky, slimy, stinky, or deadly, but all of these natural chemical weapons give the animals that use them an amazing defense.

Wild FACT If you are super brave, you can actually eat hagfish slime! Since it is made up of mostly sugars, you can bake with it. It can also be used instead of eggs in cooking.

Humans have known about chemical defenses in the animal world for many, many years. Over time, they learned how useful a chemical can be for defense. Early humans used animal poisons on spears to hunt.

Since World War I (1914–1918), chemicals have been used during battle. These weapons are usually liquid or gas. Many of them are often hard to see. These chemicals can cause terrible destruction. As science has changed, chemical weapons have gotten even more powerful.

Today, they are a bigger threat than ever. They are often called weapons of mass destruction (WMDs) because they can kill or injure a large number of people at one time. Militaries and governments have had to learn new ways to defend against chemical weapons. Most countries have laws that make these weapons illegal. Unfortunately, they are still made in some places.

the animal world, bright colors warn predators that an animal is dangerous. With chemical weapons, there is usually no such warning. Early in the 20th century, smell was usually the only way to know that dangerous chemicals were in the area. Those chemicals had very strong odors. But by the time a soldier smelled the chemical in the air, it could be too late.

Today, chemical weapons may have no smell at all. To find them, soldiers or emergency workers use lasers. Lasers are slim, focused beams of light. They can be used to find even the tiniest amounts of chemicals in the air. This helps soldiers and other emergency workers find chemical weapons faster than ever before. It also means they can work from a safe distance. Then they can take quick action to keep people in the area safe from the harmful chemicals.

Soldiers wear gear to protect them during a practice chemical attack.

Glossary

abdomen—One of an insect's three body parts. The others are the head and the thorax. The abdomen is located behind the thorax. It usually contains most of the insect's organs.

amphibians—Cold-blooded animals such as frogs that can live both on land and in water.

bluff—When an animal tricks another into thinking it is bigger, stronger, or scarier than it really is.

burrows—Tunnel-like animal homes under the snow or ground.

camouflage—When an animal uses its appearance or color to blend in with its surroundings.

captivity—An animal environment controlled by humans, as opposed to being in the wild.

defense—Protection against an attack.

diurnal—Being active during the day and resting at night.

glands—Small structures in the body that produce a substance such as venom or sweat.

mammals—Animals with hair or fur. They usually give birth to live young, are warm-blooded, and can feed their young with milk from their own bodies.

mites—Tiny spider-like animals that live on the bodies of other plants and animals.

nocturnal—Being active at night and at rest during the day.

pheromones—Chemicals produced by animals that give off a scent and send messages to other animals.

predator—An animal that hunts and eats other animals.

prey—An animal that is a food source for other animals.

reservoir—A part of the body that holds fluids.

toxic—Poisonous.

venom—A substance produced by certain animals such as snakes. It becomes toxic when injected into a victim, usually through biting.

Further Reading

Books

Branzei, Sylvia. *Animal Grossology.* New York: Price Stern Sloan, 2004.

Fridell, Ron. *The Search for Poison-Dart Frogs.* Danbury, Conn.: Franklin Watts, 2002.

Singer, Marilyn. *What Stinks?* Plain City, OH: Darby Creek Pub., 2006.

Souza, D.M. *Packed with Poison!: Deadly Animal Defenses.* Minneapolis, MN: Millbrook Press, 2006.

Internet Addresses

Journal of Young Investigators: Hagfish Aren't So Horrible After All
http://www.jyi.org/volumes/volume5/issue7/features/lee.html

National Geographic: Skunk
http://animals.nationalgeographic.com/animals/mammals/skunk.html

Zoo Friends: The Ark Files—Toxic Shock
http://www.zoofriends.org.au/childrens_activities/articles/toxic_shock.html

Index